ENCOUNTER *the One*

WHO GIVES YOU PURPOSE

AND PEACE IN A

CRAZY WORLD

PARTICIPANT'S GUIDE

MATT FRY

Most CHARISMA HOUSE BOOK GROUP products are available at special quantity discounts for bulk purchase for sales promotions, premiums, fund-raising, and educational needs. For details, write Charisma House Book Group, 600 Rinehart Road, Lake Mary, Florida 32746, or telephone (407) 333-0600.

I AM PARTICIPANT'S GUIDE by Matt Fry
Published by Charisma House
Charisma Media/Charisma House Book Group
600 Rinehart Road
Lake Mary, Florida 32746
www.charismahouse.com

Unless otherwise noted, all Scripture quotations are taken from the Holy Bible, New Living Translation, copyright © 1996, 2004, 2007. Used by permission of Tyndale House Publishers, Inc., Wheaton, IL 60189. All rights reserved.

Scripture quotations marked ESV are from the Holy Bible, English Standard Version. Copyright © 2001 by Crossway Bibles, a division of Good News Publishers. Used by permission.

Scripture quotations marked KJV are from the King James Version of the Bible.

Scripture quotations marked MEV are from the Modern English Version. Copyright © 2014 by Military Bible Association. Used by permission. All rights reserved.

Scripture quotations marked NIV are taken from the Holy Bible, New International Version®, NIV®. Copyright © 1973, 1978, 1984, 2011 by Biblica, Inc.™ Used by permission of Zondervan. All rights reserved worldwide. www.zondervan.com. The "NIV" and "New International Version" are trademarks registered in the United States Patent and Trademark Office by Biblica, Inc.™

Cover design by Lisa Rae McClure
Design Director: Justin Evans

Visit the author's website at mattfry.com.

Library of Congress Cataloging-in-Publication Data:
An application to register this book for cataloging has been submitted to the Library of Congress.
International Standard Book Number: 978-1-62999-129-0
E-book ISBN: 978-1-62999-451-2

While the author has made every effort to provide accurate Internet addresses at the time of publication, neither the publisher nor the author assumes any responsibility for errors or for changes that occur after publication.

17 18 19 20 21 — 987654321
Printed in the United States of America

Contents

Introduction.....................................ix

How to Use This Participant's Guide xi

Session 1....................................... 1
    God Is the Great I Am
    Are You Satisfied?

Session 2.....................................19
    Do You Feel Lost?
    Do You Know What You Are Looking For?

Session 3.....................................39
    Do You Know Whom You Can Trust?
    Do You Need Power?

Session 4.....................................57
    Do You Need More of God?
    Are You Connected?

Session 5.....................................75
    Do You Know Who You Are?

Introduction

I AM EXCITED THAT you are taking this journey through the principles in *I Am*. Let me encourage you not only to complete this participant's guide personally but also to study this material with others in a small group. Taking the time to study and discuss with others helps us to better apply the information to our lives. As you meet together in a small group, others may discover and share an aspect of the lesson that you may not have seen. I believe that by studying the principles in the *I Am Participant's Guide*, you will gain a deeper understanding of God's Word and His promises.

By choosing to join in this study, you have taken a very important step forward in looking to God for the answers to life's challenges and struggles. It is by getting to know the great I Am that we find the answers we seek. The key to overcoming our challenges and living out God's purpose for our lives is in having a fresh encounter with an awesome God and discovering who He truly is.

God made each of us individually and purposefully, and He invites us to interact with Him personally—to have a unique experience reflective of our relationship with Him. Our goal is not to seek a specific type of experience with I Am but simply to seek God. When we seek God, we will experience Him, and we will find that He is more than enough to meet any challenge we will face.

Our prayer is that by participating in this study, you will discover that God is everything you need—no matter what you are dealing with, no matter what the enemy may throw at you—and receive the courage to keep moving forward.

When you understand what God means when He says "I am," it will change everything. As you personally experience each of the powerful "I am" declarations Jesus made in the Gospel of John, you will discover more deeply what an amazing God we serve and embrace the significant purpose He has for your life. So let's encounter the One who gives us purpose and peace in a crazy world.

How to Use This Participant's Guide

THIS PARTICIPANT'S GUIDE is a tool to help you deepen your faith by exploring the principles in *I Am: Encounter the One Who Gives You Purpose and Peace in a Crazy World*. It is divided into five sessions and is designed to be used with my companion video series, which can be downloaded or viewed at www.encounterthegreatiam.com. A free leader's guide is available for download at the same link.

Each session corresponds with specific chapters in *I Am*, and I recommend that you read those chapters before you begin the session. The corresponding chapters are noted on the opening page of each session.

Each session includes several questions for you to think about and respond to. Ideally these questions would be discussed in a small-group setting, where you can hear how God is moving in others' lives as they work through the lessons. At the end of the discussion questions is a "Make It Personal" section that includes several promises from God's Word for you to speak over your life. I encourage you to think about these declarations and consider whether anything is keeping you from embracing them as a reality in your life.

In the final section, "Declare Who You Are in Christ," are statements for you to declare during the week. I will discuss the declarations at length in session 5, but from the start you should speak the promises of God over your life daily. If you do, I believe that your life will be changed by the end of this study. God's Word is true, and the more you remind yourself of what it says, the more it will transform your heart and mind.

Take some time to share your heart in these pages and with those in your small group. Be honest with God and with one another. James 5:16 says, "Confess your sins to each other and pray for each other so that you may be healed." God wants to use this time to move in your life and bring you into a brighter future. My prayer is that as you journey through this study, you will begin to live the rich, fulfilling life God desires for you.

God Is the Great I Am

—

Are You Satisfied?

To get the most out of this material, read the introduction and chapter 1 of *I Am* before you begin.

ONE OF THE BIGGEST challenges we face in this crazy, mixed-up world is trying to answer the question "Who am I?" If you are struggling to believe you matter or are feeling unworthy of the gifts you are given and the love you receive, answering this question can seem impossible. You might be wondering how God could love you and want to provide for you.

The most fundamental thing to understand is that no matter what you've gone through, God is still faithful, and He is good. God loves you, He is pursuing you, and He still has a purpose for your life no matter how much you've messed it up. As you go through this video series, you will begin to discover this truth: *When I encounter the great I Am, that's when I discover who I am.* Once you know who you are, you will know your purpose and live it fully.

Session 1 introduces us to the great I Am and what it means to be satisfied by His love and grace. As you begin this study, answer the following questions to determine where you are starting from and what you might be able to get out of this experience.

1. Do you feel as if you are living with a purpose to your life? Take some time to write down the things you are passionate about. What are some of your hobbies,

interests, or things you like to do when you get some free time?

_____

_____

_____

_____

2. When we begin to discover God's purpose, life is not always easy. What are some of the challenges you have already faced in getting to where you are now?

_____

_____

_____

_____

Watch the session 1 video.

God Is the Great I Am

"I Am Who I Am. Say this to the people of Israel: I Am has sent me to you." God also said to Moses, "Say this to the people of Israel: Yahweh, the God of your ancestors—the God of Abraham, the God of Isaac, and the God of Jacob—has sent me to you. This is my eternal name, my name to remember for all generations."

—Exodus 3:14–15, emphasis added

You might be wondering, "What exactly does it mean for God to say, 'I Am Who I Am'? How does that help me discover who I am?" God is the beginning and end, and everything in between. In Him you will find all you need to be fulfilled and find your purpose. But that only comes when you have a fresh encounter with God. That means connecting with God on a different level than you have in the past. It means understanding how much He loves you and how much He wants for your life, in a way that removes your doubt and insecurity. It causes you to find confidence in what you are called to do, knowing in your heart that because He has called you, He will equip you and be with you every step of the way.

We often let messages from the enemy interfere with our ability to have a fresh encounter with God, or we let the enemy cloud the messages we get from God. Answer the following questions to help you figure out what is keeping you from having a fresh encounter with God so that you can work to remove those obstacles.

1. Have you felt insecurities as Moses did, doubting your purpose and wondering if you are on the right path? Write down any negative thoughts, things you tell yourself that are keeping you from realizing your purpose. Then beside them write down what you think God might tell you instead.

Negative Things I Tell Myself	What God Would Say

2. Have you ever had a fresh encounter with God? How did it feel? What did you discover through it? If not, what do you think has kept you from having an encounter with Him?

_____

_____

_____

_____

3. What have you learned from watching the video that you can do to draw closer to God and discover the purpose He has for you?

_____

_____

_____

_____

ARE YOU SATISFIED?

Jesus replied, "I am the bread of life. Whoever comes to me will never be hungry again. Whoever believes in me will never be thirsty."

—JOHN 6:35

One of the great blessings we receive from a fresh encounter with God is a true sense of satisfaction and fulfillment. We find our value and self-esteem in who God made us to be rather than the things the world says we should be in order to be important or special. God's love for us is all that is necessary to make us worthy.

You might be basing your self-esteem on how popular you are, your physical appearance, the size of your bank account, or your title at work. Pastor Matt described his own experience with this in the video. His identity had been rooted in the job he had, and when that job went away, he wasn't sure who he was anymore—until he realized his identity was in God, and God alone. The following questions will help you determine if you've been basing your self-worth on something other than who you are in Christ.

1. Have you ever asked yourself, "Who am I?" Have you struggled to find your destiny, to figure out your place in the world, or to feel as if you matter? Explain what you were going through and what kind of answers you discovered.

   _____

   _____

   _____

   _____

2. Do you believe that God loves you and wants to provide for you? If you are struggling, try to imagine how God might be working behind the scenes to make good come of your circumstances. Write down a situation

you are dealing with from your perspective, and then make a list of ways God could bring good from it. Once you've identified God's goodness in your circumstances, write down how God's greatness is impacting this situation. Then remind yourself that He is greater than anything you will face.

_____

_____

_____

_____

3. How much of your sense of worth and value—your identity—comes from something external? In what areas of your life are you placing your significance? What would happen to your sense of worth if something happened to them?

_____

_____

_____

_____

God is I Am. That is His forever name. He always has been and always will be. He is all you need!

Only Jesus Satisfies

The testimonies from Owen and Pat reveal a lot about how the way we see ourselves affects the relationship we have with God. Let the questions below help you draw inspiration from their stories.

1. In the video we heard Owen say he could either make Marfan syndrome his excuse or his purpose. So he decided to make it his purpose. What inspiration can you draw from that statement for your own life?

   _____

   _____

   _____

   _____

2. Do you recognize some of your own behaviors in what Pat described about her journey to know Christ and discover her purpose? What might be missing in your life? What lessons do you see for yourself in her story?

   _____

   _____

   _____

   _____

**When I encounter the great I Am,
that's when I discover who I am.**

Make It Personal

At the close of the video segment I asked you to join me in speaking God's Word over our lives. Use the space provided to reflect on what the following declarations mean to you:

Jesus is the Bread of Life.

_____

_____

_____

_____

_____

Jesus is all I need.

_____

_____

_____

_____

_____

I am completely satisfied by the God of the overflow.

_____

_____

_____

_____

_____

My identity is not in my job, what I have, or where I went to school.

_____

_____

_____

_____

_____

My identity is in Jesus.

_____

_____

_____

_____

_____

Declare Who You Are in Christ

Take a few minutes each day this week to declare who you are in Christ. If you find it difficult to believe what you are declaring, ask God to show you how to embrace that promise in your daily life.

Day 1

Declare: "I am full and complete, lacking nothing."

> For in Christ all the fullness of the Deity lives in bodily form, and in Christ you have been brought to fullness. He is the head over every power and authority.
>
> —COLOSSIANS 2:9–10, NIV; ALSO SEE
> 2 PETER 1:3

> *I thank You, God, that You are not just the God of enough, but You are the God of more than enough! I declare that You are an "above and beyond" God, and I will live an "above and beyond" life for You.*

Day 2

Declare: "I am free."

> So if the Son sets you free, you are truly free.
>
> —JOHN 8:36; ALSO SEE GALATIANS 5:1;
> ROMANS 8:2

I thank You, God, that I no longer live in past regret and failure, but You have set me free to have an amazing future.

Day 3

Declare: "I am healed."

He forgives all my sins and heals all my diseases.

—Psalm 103:3

I thank You, God, that because of what You have done for me, I can be healed spiritually, physically, and emotionally.

Day 4

Declare: "I am an heir of God and coheir with Christ."

And since we are his children, we are his heirs. In fact, together with Christ we are heirs of God's glory. But if we are to share his glory, we must also share his suffering.

—Romans 8:17; also see Galatians 3:29

I thank You, God, that I inherit everything of Your kingdom as a child of God.

Day 5

Declare: "I am blessed in the heavenly realm with every spiritual blessing."

All praise to God, the Father of our Lord Jesus Christ, who has blessed us with every spiritual blessing in the heavenly realms because we are united with Christ.

—Ephesians 1:3

Thank You, God, for blessing me with every spiritual blessing!

Day 6

Declare: "I am whole."

He personally carried our sins in his body on the cross so that we can be dead to sin and live for what is right. By his wounds you are healed.

—1 Peter 2:24; also see Mark 10:52, kjv;
Acts 3:16

I thank You, God, that I am a whole and complete person. I declare that Christ is enough for me.

NOTES

NOTES

_____

_____

_____

_____

_____

_____

_____

_____

_____

_____

_____

_____

_____

_____

_____

_____

Do You Feel Lost?

—

Do You Know What You Are Looking For?

To GET THE most out
of this material, read
chapters 2 and 3 in *I
Am* before you begin.

*I*N THIS SESSION we will discuss how feeling lost has an impact on our lives and our walk with God. When we feel directionless and don't know where we are headed, we often end up making decisions that lead to trouble. Maybe you have even made choices that seemed like the right ones at the time, but you ended up disappointed because the decision didn't pan out as you expected.

In this session we will explore ways to know whether you are on the path God has laid out for you, or you are chasing something He didn't intend for your life. We will discuss how to discern the direction God wants you to take, as well as which doors to open and what you should do once you walk through them.

1. Feeling lost and without direction is confusing. Everything seems so much more overwhelming when you don't know where you are going. Do you know where you are headed, and are you OK with that direction?

   _____

   _____

   _____

   _____

2. The paths we travel in life aren't always the ones God wants for us, even though they may not necessarily be bad. Have you found what you are looking for in life? Is it truly what God made you to do?

_____

_____

_____

_____

Watch the session 2 video.

Do You Feel Lost?

> Jesus spoke to the people once more and said, "I am the light of the world. If you follow me, you won't have to walk in darkness, because you will have the light that leads to life."
>
> —John 8:12

If you feel you are wandering aimlessly and having a hard time finding something to lead you in the right direction, you are not alone. We all go through those times. It is common for us to go chasing after people or possessions that aren't ultimately going to lead us to freedom and fulfillment.

Jesus declared that He is the light, and you can trust Him to lead you. You might be wondering how to be sure the guidance you are getting is really from God. This feeling may be especially powerful if you are doubting your judgment because you have followed paths in the past that seemed right but didn't turn out well. It can be hard to discern God's desires over your own, especially if what you want isn't obviously wrong or harmful.

There are three tried-and-true ways to know if you are in line with God's will:

1. Pray, repeatedly if necessary, and God will reveal Himself to you.

2. Search His Word, where He has given us instruction for how we should live.

3. Seek godly counsel. Ask someone you trust who honors God in his or her words and actions.

These three steps should set you in the right direction. Use the following questions to explore the areas of your life where you feel lost and how God can help you find your way.

1. Think of a time when you got lost driving and couldn't get your GPS to help you find your way. What emotions did you feel when you realized you were going the wrong way? Have you ever felt that way in your personal life? How did it affect the other areas of your life and health?

_____

_____

_____

_____

2. What are some of the poor choices you made when you felt lost? Why do you think you made those decisions? In hindsight, what would you do differently?

_____

_____

_____

_____

3. How long did it take you to get back on course? What helped you find your way? What verses in the Bible have been helpful to you when you've felt lost?

_____

_____

_____

_____

Do You Know What You Are Looking For?

I am the door. If anyone enters through Me, he will be saved and will go in and out and find pasture.

—John 10:9, mev

Answering the question "What are you looking for?" can be really challenging, especially if you are feeling lost. Sometimes we are lost because we don't know what we need. We may want a door that will lead to happiness and fulfillment, but we don't have a clue what that means.

As you look for opportunities in life, it is important to be able to determine what is a *good* opportunity and what is a *God* opportunity. The three steps we covered previously for determining what is God's will are useful in this process as well. But no matter what you are facing, Jesus is the door that opens up to all the amazing things God has planned for us here on earth and that await us in heaven. Use the following questions to help you develop a plan for evaluating the doors you encounter in life.

1. Have you ever opened a door of opportunity that took you in the wrong direction? Were there signs that could have let you know it was the wrong door to walk through? Did you ignore those signs? If so, why?

   _____

   _____

   _____

   _____

2. Not all wrong doors lead to bad situations or even look wrong. Have you ever been faced with a decision where more than one option seemed good and sent from God? How did you choose which door to open?

   _____

   _____

_____

_____

3. What tools do you use to determine what is a *good* opportunity and what is a *God* opportunity? Who are some of the people in your life you trust for guidance? What books do you read to help you make decisions? Are there specific verses from the Bible that lead you? Do you take time to pray for direction?

_____

_____

_____

_____

Trust in the Lord with all your heart; do not depend on your own understanding. Seek his will in all you do, and he will show you which path to take. —Proverbs 3:5-6

With Jesus You Are Never Lost

In the testimonies from Charlie and Brad, we see great illustrations of the impact feeling lost has on our lives and how to get back on track.

1. Have you spent much of your life, as Charlie did, getting lost by taking wrong turns? If so, what have you learned from those detours? If not, how have you avoided those wrong turns?

   _____

   _____

   _____

   _____

   _____

2. What about the wrong path can make us think it is the right one? How can a person get off the wrong path and back onto the right one, as Brad did?

   _____

   _____

   _____

   _____

   _____

JESUS IS THE ANSWER

Jill's story in *I Am* ("Jesus Is the Answer," in chapter 3) is a great example of understanding the difference between *good* opportunities and *God* opportunities.

1. Have you ever opened a door thinking it was the right one but it actually led you to the wrong place? If so, what did you do? What are some ways God has brought good out of mistakes and detours you have made in life?

   _____

   _____

   _____

   _____

2. What have your experiences making wrong turns taught you about how to discern where God really wants you to go?

   _____

   _____

   _____

   _____

   _____

Is it a *good* opportunity or a *God* opportunity?

Make It Personal

At the close of the video segment I asked you to join me in speaking God's Word over our lives. Use the space provided to reflect on what the following declarations mean to you:

Jesus is the light of the world and the light to my path.

_____

_____

_____

_____

_____

_____

_____

_____

_____

Jesus is the door that will lead me to the purpose God has for my life.

_____

_____

_____

_____

_____

_____

_____

_____

_____

_____

When I feel lost, I can turn to God, and God will lead me where He wants me to go.

_____

_____

_____

_____

_____

_____

_____

_____

Declare Who You Are in Christ

Take a few minutes each day this week to declare who you are in Christ. If you find it difficult to believe what you are declaring, ask God to show you how to embrace that promise in your daily life.

Day 1

Declare: "I am a new creation—the old life is gone!"

> This means that anyone who belongs to Christ has become a new person. The old life is gone; a new life has begun!
>
> —2 Corinthians 5:17;
> also see Colossians 3:10

I thank You, God, that I am a new creation. You are the only One who can create and make something or someone new. I declare that my old life is gone and You are doing a new thing in me!

Day 2

Declare: "I am His treasured possession."

> "Now if you will obey me and keep my covenant, you will be my own special treasure from among all the peoples on earth; for all the earth belongs to me. And you will be my kingdom of priests,

my holy nation." This is the message you must give to the people of Israel.

—Exodus 19:5–6;
also see 2 Corinthians 4:7

I thank You, God, that I have value in Your eyes and I am Your treasured possession.

Day 3

Declare: "I am precious to God. I am being built into a spiritual house."

You are coming to Christ, who is the living cornerstone of God's temple. He was rejected by people, but he was chosen by God for great honor. And you are living stones that God is building into his spiritual temple. What's more, you are his holy priests. Through the mediation of Jesus Christ, you offer spiritual sacrifices that please God.

—1 Peter 2:4–5

I thank You, God, that You don't see me as just a number, but as someone who is precious to You.

Day 4

Declare: "I am His ambassador."

And all of this is a gift from God, who brought us back to himself through Christ. And God has given us this task of reconciling people to him. For God was in Christ, reconciling the world to himself, no longer counting people's sins against them. And he gave us this wonderful message of reconciliation. So we are Christ's ambassadors; God is making his appeal through us. We speak for Christ when we plead, "Come back to God!" For God made Christ, who never sinned, to be the offering for our sin, so that we could be made right with God through Christ.

—2 Corinthians 5:18–21

I thank You, God, that I have the privilege of being Your ambassador, sharing Your love and good news with the world.

Day 5

Declare: "I am a warrior for Christ."

Endure suffering along with me, as a good soldier of Christ Jesus. Soldiers don't get tied up in the affairs of civilian life, for then they cannot please the officer who enlisted them.

—2 Timothy 2:3–4; also see Psalm 18:32–42

I thank You, God, that I am a mighty warrior for You. I declare that I will fight the good fight through prayer and by shining Your light to others.

Day 6

Declare: "I am a citizen of God's kingdom."

> Since we are receiving a Kingdom that is unshakable, let us be thankful and please God by worshiping him with holy fear and awe.
>
> —HEBREWS 12:28; ALSO SEE PHILIPPIANS 3:20

I thank You, Lord, that this earth is not my home, but my eternal home is in heaven, and I am a citizen of Your kingdom!

NOTES

_____

_____

_____

_____

_____

_____

_____

_____

_____

_____

_____

_____

_____

_____

NOTES

_____

_____

_____

_____

_____

_____

_____

_____

_____

_____

_____

_____

_____

_____

_____

3

Do You Know Whom You Can Trust?

—

Do You Need Power?

To GET THE most out
of this material, read
chapters 4 and 5 in *I
Am* before you begin.

*Y*OU MIGHT NOT THINK your ability to trust others has an impact on discovering who you are, but having your trust betrayed can cause you to question your own judgment. It can even make you feel as though you don't have control over important areas of your life. These feelings can also cause you to doubt your faith in God and lead you to try to control areas of your life that should be placed in His hands.

In this session we will talk about how you can discern whom to trust and find the faith to fully put your trust in God. By doing so, you will learn how to surrender control to Him over the big and the small things, having full confidence in His ability to take care of your needs and lead you in your decision making.

1. Learning to trust is one of the biggest challenges we face. When someone breaks that trust, it affects us deeply. Whom in your life do you trust, and why?

   _____

   _____

   _____

   _____

2. We all need to feel we have power over situations in our lives. When we feel powerless, we sometimes feel everything is out of control. What makes you feel the most powerless?

_____

_____

_____

_____

Watch the session 3 video.

Do You Know Whom You Can Trust?

> I am the good shepherd. The good shepherd sacrifices his life for the sheep.
>
> —John 10:11

If you have ever put your trust in someone who ended up letting you down—maybe a spouse who left you, a business partner who embezzled from you, or a teacher or coach who abused you—you know that these types of devastating experiences can impact the rest of your life. When a betrayal such as this happens, you may think you will never be able to trust anyone again. You might even wonder where God was when that painful event occurred.

It may not feel this way in the middle of those circumstances, but Jesus said He would never leave us or forsake us, and that is the truth. People will let us down. Because they are free to make their own choices, sometimes people choose things that harm us. God may not stop them from making those choices, but you can count on Him to be there to help you through the outcomes.

God is there for you to lean on, and He will guide you to restoration. Use the following questions to examine ways you have felt betrayed and how those situations might have affected your ability to trust others or even to trust God.

1. When you feel betrayed, how does it impact your other relationships and your ability to trust?

   _____

   _____

   _____

   _____

2. When people betray your trust, are you able to forgive them and trust them again? If so, what do they have to do to regain your trust? If not, what would it take for you to be willing to trust again?

   _____

   _____

   _____

   _____

3. Do you believe God wants us to trust even those who have betrayed us? What does God give us to help us have confidence in deciding whom to trust?

_____

_____

_____

_____

Do You Need Power?

I am the resurrection and the life. Anyone who believes in me will live, even after dying.

—John 11:25

The inability to trust often leads to feelings of powerlessness, and it can keep us from turning our cares over to God. We find ourselves wanting to hold on to things we shouldn't be worried about and that really aren't in our control because we think doing so will give us power over those situations.

There are so many obstacles and challenges in life that we are powerless to change on our own, and trying to control people, situations, and outcomes only makes a bigger mess. But God's power will help you overcome these difficulties and disappointments in life. The following questions will help you determine where you are trying to control the uncontrollable in your life and begin to turn those concerns over to God.

1. Have you ever found it difficult to trust someone who holds power over you? How did that make you feel (i.e., angry, vulnerable, afraid)?

    _____

    _____

    _____

    _____

2. Do you often find yourself relying on your own abilities and being unwilling to surrender any power to other people? What problems has that created for you?

    _____

    _____

    _____

3. Have you ever been able to surrender yourself to God and let His power fill you? If not, why? If so, what difference did you notice between what you were able to accomplish in your own power and what you could do through God's power?

    _____

    _____

    _____

    _____

People will fail you, but Jesus will never fail you.

YOU CAN ALWAYS TRUST GOD

Amanda's testimony reveals the impact that broken trust can have on every area of our lives and how relationships can be restored when we trust God to lead us.

1. Have you ever faced an issue that caused you to struggle with trust? What did you find yourself putting your trust in as a result?

   _____

   _____

   _____

   _____

2. Do you ever find it hard to trust God? Why or why not?

   _____

   _____

   _____

   _____

JESUS IS YOUR STRENGTH WHEN YOU FEEL HELPLESS

Paul struggled with a lack of control over many aspects of his life. He shows us what can happen and how God can heal the broken parts of our lives when we turn control back over to Him.

1. Have you ever felt out of control? If so, did you feel the control was taken a little at a time or all at once? How did you cope with that loss? Was your method productive?

   _____

   _____

   _____

   _____

2. Have you surrendered control to God? If so, how has your life improved since doing so? If you are holding back, in what ways has this impacted your life?

   _____

   _____

   _____

   _____

Focus on Jesus, and He will
show you how to trust the right
people at the right time.

Make It Personal

At the close of the video segment I asked you to join me in speaking God's Word over our lives. Use the space provided to reflect on what the following declarations mean to you:

Jesus is the Good Shepherd, and He will never let me down.

_____

_____

_____

_____

_____

_____

_____

_____

_____

Jesus is the resurrection and the Life, and He will fill me with abundant life.

_____

_____

_____

_____

_____

_____

_____

_____

_____

I will put my trust in God to lead me and help me make the right choices.

_____

_____

_____

_____

_____

_____

_____

_____

_____

Declare Who You Are in Christ

Take a few minutes each day this week to declare who you are in Christ. If you find it difficult to believe what you are declaring, ask God to show you how to embrace that promise in your daily life.

Day 1

Declare: "I am greatly loved by God."

> This is real love—not that we loved God, but that he loved us and sent his Son as a sacrifice to take away our sins.
>
> —1 John 4:10

I thank You, God, that You love me unconditionally, with no strings attached. You love me no matter who I am or what I've done. You love me even when I don't deserve it.

Day 2

Declare: "I am His child."

> See how very much our Father loves us, for he calls us his children, and that is what we are! But the people who belong to this world don't recognize that we are God's children because they don't know him. Dear friends, we are already

God's children, but he has not yet shown us what we will be like when Christ appears. But we do know that we will be like him, for we will see him as he really is.

—1 John 3:1–2; also see Romans 8:14–15

I thank You, God, that I am a child of the most high God! I don't have to live in fear because I know that You are my heavenly Father.

Day 3

Declare: "I am a friend of God, chosen by Him and appointed to bear good fruit."

I no longer call you slaves, because a master doesn't confide in his slaves. Now you are my friends, since I have told you everything the Father told me. You didn't choose me. I chose you. I appointed you to go and produce lasting fruit, so that the Father will give you whatever you ask for, using my name.

—John 15:15–16

Lord, I thank You that I am a friend of Yours and that when I abide in You I will bear all of the fruit of the Spirit!

Day 4

Declare: "I am sent by God."

As he spoke, he showed them the wounds in his hands and his side. They were filled with joy when they saw the Lord! Again he said, "Peace be with you. As the Father has sent me, so I am sending you." Then he breathed on them and said, "Receive the Holy Spirit. If you forgive anyone's sins, they are forgiven. If you do not forgive them, they are not forgiven."

—JOHN 20:20–23; ALSO SEE ROMANS 10:15

I thank You, God, for saving me and calling me to live my life on assignment from You to make a difference in the world.

Day 5

Declare: "I am light in the darkness."

You are the salt of the earth. But what good is salt if it has lost its flavor? Can you make it salty again? It will be thrown out and trampled underfoot as worthless. You are the light of the world—like a city on a hilltop that cannot be hidden. No one lights a lamp and then puts it under a basket. Instead, a lamp is placed on a stand, where it gives light to everyone in the house. In the same way, let your good deeds shine out for all to see, so that everyone will praise your heavenly Father.

—MATTHEW 5:13–16; ALSO SEE EPHESIANS 5:8

I thank You, God, that I can shine Your light in the dark places, and because of Your goodness to me, others will see how awesome You are.

Day 6

Declare: "I am more than a conqueror."

No, in all these things we are more than conquerors through Him who loved us.

—Romans 8:37, mev; also see
1 Corinthians 15:57

I thank You, God, that I am more than a conqueror and have power over the enemy, in Jesus's name. Nothing can stop me from living out Your plan for my life.

NOTES

_____

_____

_____

_____

_____

_____

_____

_____

_____

_____

_____

_____

_____

_____

NOTES

_____

_____

_____

_____

_____

_____

_____

_____

_____

_____

_____

_____

_____

_____

Do You Need
More of God?

—

Are You Connected?

To GET THE most out of this material, read chapters 6 and 7 in *I Am* before you begin.

*A*S YOU DIG DEEPER into discovering who you are and who God made you to be, one of the things that will help the most is to feel connected to the people and the blessings in your life. When we feel disconnected, it affects our perspective and ability to see beyond our circumstances. When we are connected to others, that network of support can help us find solutions for moving forward and sometimes simply find hope for the future.

Our connection to God is of even greater importance than our connection to the people in our lives. You might be connected to God by your faith in Him but not feeling His presence in your life. This might be a sign that you need more of God. Going to church and participating in activities there isn't enough. Even reading the Bible and praying may not give you as much of God as you need if you are just going through the motions.

This session will help you learn more about the connections you can have with those around you and with God. Using the following questions, begin examining which relationships are enriching your life and which might be distracting you from your purpose and relationship with God.

1. Making connections with those around us—God, friends, family, coworkers—is an essential part of feeling we are living a meaningful life. How strong are your connections?

_____

_____

_____

_____

2. When we are feeling disconnected, regardless of which relationship we are feeling disconnected from, the reason can always be traced back to how much of God's presence we are allowing into our lives. Are you getting as much of God as you need?

_____

_____

_____

_____

Watch the session 4 video.

Do You Need More of God?

I am the way, the truth, and the life. No one can come to the Father except through me.

—John 14:6, emphasis added

When we face challenges and are searching for answers, there is no shortage of opinions and advice on what to do. But none of these will get us where we need to be if we aren't letting God lead us. And the only way to do that is to know God personally.

Having more of God in your life is not as easy as it sounds. You may think all it takes is going to church more often and maybe memorizing more verses of the Bible. But it takes more. It means changing the way we live so we honor God with every thought and action and continually seek His will. Whether you grew up in church, are just beginning your relationship with God, or have never prayed before in your life, drawing closer to God and understanding the ways He can work in your life are essential.

Use the following questions to evaluate how you may or may not be inviting more of God into your life and what you can do to get more of Him.

1. What do you do to cultivate your relationship with God? Do you do anything at all? Do you think going to church on Sundays, or even just on the holidays, is enough?

_____

_____

_____

_____

2. What does it mean to you that Jesus said, "I am the way, the truth, and the life"? What does that tell you about the kind of relationship God wants to have with you?

_____

_____

_____

_____

3. Are there areas of your life that would benefit from having more of God in them? How can you invite God into those spaces? How do you think it would impact those parts of your life if God filled them?

_____

_____

_____

_____

ARE YOU CONNECTED?

Yes, *I am the vine*; you are the branches. Those who remain in me, and I in them, will produce much fruit. For apart from me you can do nothing.

—JOHN 15:5, EMPHASIS ADDED

We all go through times in our lives when we struggle to feel connected to the things and people who matter and question whether we are making the right choices. Maybe you've moved to a new city for work or school and feel lonely and cut off. Sometimes you don't even need to relocate to feel displaced—you might be surrounded by friends and family and still feel alone. This happens when we aren't connected to God in a way that restores and fulfills us.

Our connections to people can be healthy and strengthen our relationship with God, but if we don't have a strong connection with Him, they can serve to separate us from Him and cause confusion. Good relationships are important, but it is our connection to God that feeds us with the kind of strength and love that will sustain us through any circumstances we face. Use the following questions to determine what kinds of connections you have and whether they are leading you *toward* or *away from* God.

1. What are the most important connections in your life? What do you do to strengthen them and make sure you stay connected?

_____

_____

_____

_____

_____

2. Have you lost your connection with certain people in your life? Why has that happened? What can you do to restore those connections?

_____

_____

_____

_____

_____

_____

3. What about your relationship with God? What is the status of that connection? Do you feel your other relationships are more important or need more care than your relationship with Him? What link do you see between how your earthly relationships are going and how your relationship with God is going?

_____

_____

_____

_____

_____

_____

We must surrender ourselves to Jesus, who is the Way, the Truth, and the Life, because we can't do life alone, and we can't achieve salvation alone.

When Life Gets Tough, Press Into God

Anisa's testimony confirms that the worst thing we can do when we feel the strain of difficult times is turn inward and pull away from God. That is when we should be drawing closer to Him.

1. Have you ever found yourself away from God and needing more of Him? If so, what was it that caused you to pull away in the first place? Did pulling away make things better or worse? If you haven't found yourself feeling distant from God, how have you kept your connection close?

   _____

   _____

   _____

   _____

2. Are you plugged into a church? If so, how has attending church affected the way you connect with God and others? If not, what is keeping you from seeking a church home?

_____

_____

_____

_____

Through Jesus's Love We All Are Connected

Matt W.'s letter ("We All Are Connected Through Jesus's Love," in chapter 7 of *I Am*) is affirmation that being part of a church family and being involved in others' lives has an enormous impact on our relationship with God and helps to deepen that connection.

1. Why is having a connection with God so important? What about connections to strong Christian leaders and a faith community?

_____

_____

_____

_____

2. In what ways do those connections deepen your impact on others?

_____

_____

_____

_____

- -

Healing comes when we connect to God and to one another relationally.

- -

Make It Personal

At the close of the video segment I asked you to join me in speaking God's Word over our lives. Use the space provided to reflect on what the following declarations mean to you:

Jesus shows me the way to go; I will follow Him.

_____

_____

_____

_____

_____

Jesus is the Truth; I will listen to Him.

_____

_____

_____

_____

_____

Jesus is the Life; I will live for Him.

_____

_____

_____

_____

_____

As the vine connects to the branch, I will connect to You, God, through a relationship with Jesus. I need You.

_____

_____

_____

_____

_____

Declare Who You Are in Christ

Take a few minutes each day this week to declare who you are in Christ. If you find it difficult to believe what you are declaring, ask God to show you how to embrace that promise in your daily life.

Day 1

Declare: "I am chosen to be part of a royal priesthood, a holy nation set apart for God."

> But you are not like that, for you are a chosen people. You are royal priests, a holy nation, God's very own possession. As a result, you can show others the goodness of God, for he called you out of the darkness into his wonderful light.
>
> —1 Peter 2:9; also see Revelation 5:10;
> Ephesians 1:3–4

Thank You, God, for choosing me to be royalty.

Day 2

Declare: "I am His radiant bride; I am without spot or wrinkle."

> For husbands, this means love your wives, just as Christ loved the church. He gave up his life for her to make her holy and clean, washed by the cleansing of God's word. He did this to present

her to himself as a glorious church without a spot or wrinkle or any other blemish. Instead, she will be holy and without fault. In the same way, husbands ought to love their wives as they love their own bodies. For a man who loves his wife actually shows love for himself. No one hates his own body but feeds and cares for it, just as Christ cares for the church. And we are members of his body. As the Scriptures say, "A man leaves his father and mother and is joined to his wife, and the two are united into one." This is a great mystery, but it is an illustration of the way Christ and the church are one.

—EPHESIANS 5:25–32; ALSO SEE
2 CORINTHIANS 11:2

I thank You, God, that You are coming again for Your church and that as part of Your family I am a radiant bride who is clean and holy!

Day 3

Declare: "I am significant."

All of you together are Christ's body, and each of you is a part of it.

—1 CORINTHIANS 12:27;
ALSO SEE ROMANS 12:4–5

I thank You, God, that You didn't call me to live a normal life but give me the power to live a significant life for Your glory.

Day 4

Declare: "I am wanted."

Come close to God, and God will come close to you. Wash your hands, you sinners; purify your hearts, for your loyalty is divided between God and the world.

—JAMES 4:8

I thank You, God, that not only do You love me, but You also like me. You want me to be in Your presence. I declare that I will draw closer to You as You draw closer to me.

Day 5

Declare: "I am called by name."

God decided in advance to adopt us into his own family by bringing us to himself through Jesus Christ. This is what he wanted to do, and it gave him great pleasure. So we praise God for the glorious grace he has poured out on us who belong to his dear Son. He is so rich in kindness and grace that he purchased our freedom with the blood of his Son and forgave our sins. He has showered his kindness on us, along with all wisdom and understanding.

—Ephesians 1:5–8; also see Isaiah 43:1

I thank You, God, that You know my name. Not only do You save me, but You also call me to make a difference! I thank You that I can have a relationship with You that is real and personal.

Day 6

Declare: "I am a member of God's family."

So now you Gentiles are no longer strangers and foreigners. You are citizens along with all of God's holy people. You are members of God's family. Together, we are his house, built on the foundation of the apostles and the prophets. And the cornerstone is Christ Jesus himself.

—Ephesians 2:19–20;
also see Ephesians 3:15, MEV

I thank You, God, that I am not alone but that I belong to Your family.

NOTES

_____

_____

_____

_____

_____

_____

_____

_____

_____

_____

_____

_____

_____

_____

NOTES

_____

_____

_____

_____

_____

_____

_____

_____

_____

_____

_____

_____

_____

_____

_____

_____

5

Do You Know
Who You Are?

To GET THE most out
of this material, read
chapter 8 in *I Am*
before you begin.

*T*HROUGHOUT THIS STUDY we have been looking at the "I am" statements Jesus made and discovering what they mean for our lives and our relationships with God. We have examined the following questions:

- Are you satisfied?

- Do you feel lost?

- Do you know what you are looking for?

- Do you know whom you can trust?

- Do you need power?

- Do you need more of God?

- Are you connected?

The final question to answer—and the most important for discovering who you are in Christ—is, who does God say you are?

Use the following questions to begin thinking about what you have let yourself believe about who you are and how that compares with who God says you are.

1. We listen to a lot of messages from others and from ourselves about who we are that do not give us the full

picture. What are some things you have believed about yourself that didn't come from God?

_____

_____

_____

_____

_____

_____

2. God's message to us is that we are wonderfully and fearfully made by Him. What does that mean to you? Are you living that out?

_____

_____

_____

_____

_____

_____

Watch the session 5 video.

Do You Know Who You Are?

Therefore, if anyone is in Christ, he is a new creation. The old has passed away; behold, the new has come.

—2 Corinthians 5:17, esv

Our identity in God is the key to opening doors of opportunity and blessing. Knowing this also helps us close the door on fears and doubts. But even greater is the discovery of who He made each of us to be, which brings us into closer relationship with Him.

Are you asking yourself, "Who am I?" If so, you have to start answering that question by understanding who God is and what He has done for you. Once you know who He is, you will begin to find the answer to who you are. As you respond to the following questions, ask God to use them to reveal Himself and the great love He has for you.

1. Who does God say you are? What promises has He declared over your life that you need to embrace so you can live more joyfully and purposefully?

_____

_____

_____

_____

_____

2. Have you had a fresh encounter with God? What did it reveal to you about who you are and who God says you are? If you haven't had an encounter with God, what do you think is preventing that?

_____

_____

_____

_____

_____

3. Are the person God says you are and the person you believe you are the same? If not, in what ways is your understanding of yourself different?

_____

_____

_____

_____

_____

4. What can you do to bring your beliefs about yourself into alignment with who God made you to be?

_____

_____

_____

_____

_____

5. What declarations or promises from God's Word can you speak over your life to help you draw closer to God and what He wants for you?

_____

_____

_____

_____

6. What have you discovered through this study about who you are and who God wants you to be? What are you going to do to be a vessel for His glory?

_____

_____

_____

_____

When I encounter the great I Am, that's when I discover who I am.

I Am Changed; I Am Redeemed

Michelle's story is a great reminder that the hurtful and negative messages we allow into our hearts and minds are never from God and actually come from the enemy to distract us from God's purpose for our lives.

1. Have you been holding on to negative messages or hurtful experiences that may be keeping you from fulfilling God's purpose for your life? If so, why have you been unable to let go of those wounds? If not, how were you able to release those painful experiences?

   _____

   _____

   _____

   _____

2. What can you do to reject negative messages sent from the enemy to distract you from your purpose and rob you of peace and joy?

   _____

   _____

   _____

   _____

Your greatest days are ahead!

Make It Personal

Speak the following promises from God's Word over your life. Use the space provided to reflect on what those declarations mean to you:

I am greatly loved by God; I am His child.

_____

_____

_____

_____

_____

_____

_____

God has called me, and He is faithful to complete His work in my life.

_____

_____

_____

_____

_____

_____

_____

_____

I am full and complete, lacking nothing.

_____

_____

_____

_____

_____

_____

I am wanted by God. I am victorious in Him.

_____

_____

_____

_____

_____

_____

_____

Declare Who You Are in Christ

Take a few minutes each day this week to declare who you are in Christ. If you find it difficult to believe what you are declaring, ask God to show you how to embrace that promise in your daily life.

Day 1

Declare: "I am fearfully and wonderfully made by a holy God."

> Thank you for making me so wonderfully complex! Your workmanship is marvelous—how well I know it.
>
> —Psalm 139:14

> *Thank You, God, that I am not an accident. You knit me in my mother's womb. I am fearfully and wonderfully made by the Creator of the universe.*

Day 2

Declare: "I am God's masterpiece."

> For we are God's masterpiece. He has created us anew in Christ Jesus, so we can do the good things he planned for us long ago.
>
> —Ephesians 2:10

I thank You, God, that I was handcrafted by You. There is no one else in the world exactly like me. I am one of a kind, and I have a destiny.

Day 3

Declare: "I am made in the image of God."

Then God said, "Let us make human beings in our image, to be like us. They will reign over the fish in the sea, the birds in the sky, the livestock, all the wild animals on the earth, and the small animals that scurry along the ground."

—GENESIS 1:26; ALSO SEE
GENESIS 9:6; COLOSSIANS 1:27

I thank You, God, that I was made in Your image! And Your Word says in John 14:12 that we can do even greater things than You ever did!

Day 4

Declare: "I am a temple of the living God."

Don't you realize that all of you together are the temple of God and that the Spirit of God lives in you? God will destroy anyone who destroys this temple. For God's temple is holy, and you are that temple.

—1 CORINTHIANS 3:16–17; ALSO SEE
1 CORINTHIANS 6:19; 2 CORINTHIANS 6:16

Thank You, God, that my body is Your temple. I declare that I will keep it healthy for Your glory.

Day 5

Declare: "I am forgiven."

And he ordered us to preach everywhere and to testify that Jesus is the one appointed by God to be the judge of all—the living and the dead. He is the one all the prophets testified about, saying that everyone who believes in him will have their sins forgiven through his name.

—ACTS 10:42–43; ALSO SEE 1 JOHN 1:9;
ISAIAH 43:25–26; PSALM 103:12

I thank You, God, that when we confess our sins to You, You forgive us, cleanse us, and forget about our wrongdoing! Our sins are washed away forever, and we can live in freedom.

Day 6

Declare: "I am the righteousness of God."

For God made Christ, who never sinned, to be the offering for our sin, so that we could be made right with God through Christ.

—2 CORINTHIANS 5:21

I thank You, God, that You see me as righteous and holy because of what You did for me on the cross.

Bonus Declaration

Declare: "I am redeemed by God."

In him we have redemption through his blood, the forgiveness of sins, in accordance with the riches of God's grace.

—EPHESIANS 1:7, NIV

I thank You, God, that You have redeemed my life and have given me a fresh start!

NOTES

_____

_____

_____

_____

_____

_____

_____

_____

_____

_____

_____

_____

_____

_____

NOTES

_____

_____

_____

_____

_____

_____

_____

_____

_____

_____

_____

_____

_____

_____

_____

NOTES

NOTES

NOTES

NOTES

NOTES

CONNECT WITH US!

CHARISMA HOUSE

(Spiritual Growth)

Facebook.com/CharismaHouse

@CharismaHouse

Instagram.com/CharismaHouse

(Health)

Pinterest.com/CharismaHouse

(Bible)

www.mevbible.com